Blue Autumn

RENEWALS 458-4574
DATE DUE

GAYLORD			PRINTED IN U.S.A.

ALSO BY CHRISTOPHER BUCKLEY

Last Rites (Ithaca House, 1980)
Other Lives (Ithaca House, 1985)
Dust Light, Leaves (Vanderbilt, 1986)
Blossoms & Bones (Vanderbilt, 1988)

BLUE AUTUMN

poems

Christopher Buckley

Copper Beech Press

Grateful acknowledgment is made to the editors of the publications in which some of these poems first appeared, sometimes in slightly different versions: *Chiaroscuro* ("Coming Away with Something"); *Crazyhorse* ("Playing for Time," "The Lost Catechism of the Clouds"); *The Denver Quarterly* ("To Giordano Bruno in the Campo de' Fiori," "Photograph of Myself by Modigliani's Grave, Pere Lachaise, 1984") *Indiana Review* ("Extempore," "Halley's Comet from the West Coast, March 22, 1986," "Self-Portrait with Winter"); *The Missouri Review* ("Homage to Canaletto"); *The Nation* ("Giotto's 'St. Francis Preaching to the Birds'"); *Pacific Review* ("The Adulation of the Air," "*The Aborigines* in the Jardin des Plantes"); *The Pennsylvania Review* ("Old Spanish Days"); *Ploughshares* ("Another Place and Time"); *Poetry* ("Evening in Santorini," "Walking Out the Appian Way Past the Circus of Maxentius," "On the Eiffel Tower," "Clouds in Summer," "Blue Autumn," "Last Night in Akrotiri," "The Inverse Square Law of the Propagation of Light," "The Past"); *The Poetry Miscellany* ("Ars Poetica"); and *Quarterly West* ("October Visiting").

Cover: Detail from *Cycle*, © 1990 by Nadya Brown.

Thanks for grants from the Commonwealth of Pennsylvania Council on the Arts and from the State System of Higher Education of the Commonwealth of Pennsylvania, which gave me time to complete some of these poems. Thanks also to Rod Santos, Jon Veinberg, Mark Jarman, and Nadya Brown for their help with these poems and to Joseph Parisi for his consideration; special thanks to the Bread Loaf Writers' Conference and Philip Levine for revision suggestions. —C.B.

Copper Beech Press
English Department
Box 1852
Brown University
Providence, Rhode Island 02912

Library of Congress Cataloging-in-Publication Data
Buckley, Christopher, 1948 -
  Blue Autumn: poems / Christopher Buckley.
    p. cm.
  ISBN 0-914278-53-3 (alk. paper) : $9.95
  I. Title.
  PS3552.U339B54   1990
  811'.54 — dc20   89-77314
                                                            CIP

First Edition
Printed in the United States of America

CONTENTS

And beyond it, the deep blue air, that shows
Nothing, and is nowhere, and is endless.
Philip Larkin

I

COMING AWAY WITH SOMETHING

for Mark Jarman

Just before a nap, late afternoon,
I gaze up to the rust-edged sky
above which unseen birds are passing,
feeling there's some gesture I should make. . .
Incidents then are a rain of dust until
again it is my grandfather's farm,
the clearing by the big, white house,
the shade trees awash with cool air —
and my father, who was never there,
appears from behind them in a beard
he never wore, holds a piece of cardboard
I colored in my 5th year, and points
to the large, uneven words,
waiting for me to recite them aloud,
stands there blinking like an old horse.

But soon he walks off toward a building
that looms ancient and civic on the rise —
a place where gardens might be hanging
over walls, but the bricks are spare and bright
and he is gone into the sandy glare of it.
I'm left working at the cardboard as
the black letters begin to lift in flocks.

Then my mother saunters up the path
in her jodhpurs and knee-high riding boots,
and we are off to the garden to cut
pink chrysanthemums for the kitchen
where her mother drifts about the stove
and is herself a warm and lilac cloud
dusted with flour.
                    I soon forget
the ziggurat, my father the Assyrian King,
and again discover the silverware,
heavy and large in my hands —
the red plastic handles glowing
like the sun through the evening window

which pulls me back to a world
where I have forgotten how
I am expected to ask for things,
and reach for them this way.

BLUE AUTUMN

Santa Barbara, 1986

On a swing above the ivied sandstone wall
I swooped the level of the trees and twilight,
the gold-grey streaks and violet trumpet vines,
and with legs rowing up the evening air
my arms pushed wide and bird-pure
against the chill squeaking of the chains.
Here my first dreams and vague despair,
translating clouds to the heart's reward —
alone in my blue school sweater, my hands
were stuffed with the airy fabric of the sky;
wind-stung and light-lost toward the sea,
I was five years old and burning alive.

*

Giant sycamores bent back clouds half a block
from the beach. We corner-cut the wild
ivy of a vacant lot, the watery shade of palms,
snaked our way through the lemon fields'
waist-high grass, and were here and there
beneath honeysuckle and trees of tangerines,
landing at length and round about on the sand,
traipsing our high-top sneakers unceremoniously
through tide pools and running skirts of surf.

We were boys in possession of our days,
bright and slow beneath the olive boughs.
We gazed up to where, even without a cloud,
we could see air move as surely as our blood
pumped to our fingertips as we swung
limb to limb and jumped through
the daylight for all that we were worth.

*

We were green then, supple as the weeds,
and chewing thick stems of sour grass mistook
the cool acids for the stuff of our young hearts.
Oh we were immune to love, wearing home

the old school jerseys after games —
over-washed and white, the numerals bleached
grey. And ganged-up and walking down
the cypressed lanes were buoyant and carefree
for we had hit and run smartly with a knee
and forearm shiver, diving through those
hoops of air — Armour, Knapp, and Stanton
Richards gunned the bootleg and halfback
reverse for our winning score across the chalk-
dust of that once and true vainglory. . .

And though we mastered the iconography
of kickball and the Stations of the Cross,
mumbled Latin and the sorrowful mysteries
by rote, all the while our hearts churned
openly for the playing field and sun
with no second thoughts about our souls.

*

Now I jog around the lake and the birds
keep to themselves their secret about the sky.
I have moved through the air, mutable
as any leaf, seeing the wind's passion
for the golden nettle crowning eugenia,
those purple berries we threw then
after school to leave our parting marks,
our lack of contrition pronounced against
the church's sun-stropped walls.

Now, I've come full circle with the citrus trees,
with the winter light rouged along these hills —
and still I am taken with that last copper streak
of cloud in a creek pool. Wandering out,
I know nothing truer than this daylight breathing
through the lemon leaves, the radiant streaming
down of it as I walk cliffs where it's all pale
dust sent up by that wind which, like me,
wants to hold everything it couldn't help

letting go. I can tell by the way it covets
each waxy perfume of laurel and pittosporum,
each evidence of salt off the spindrift breeze.
Still, I like to be here when the wind blooms
and these ungainly eucalyptus lean out
like ghosts calling in the horizon's clouds. . .
But crows spearheaded through the coastal pines
won't let me overlook the dark, the flared
assurances of sun going dim by the evening star,
that one I bargained a faithful life away
on as a boy. Yet from that first moment
in the failing light, the complication in being
here was clear — the mountains retouched each fall
with fire, and ash sifting down as if the blind
moon had shed a rain of petals and no blessing
to sustain us finally from the dark.
                                Even so,
I am no one if not that boy still longing
for some gesture, some lift and song to ride him
out above the gloss and bay, if only for an instant
with the birds, with feathers of imagined wing
filtering dusk, that spume and flowback of days
when each passage was as evident as light,
as sure and unfinished as the sea's blue refrain.

THE ADULATION OF THE AIR

In Charleston, West Virginia,
I'm four, riding with my father
in our Oldsmobile as sun sparks shear
off the chrome, futuristic ornament
on the hood. And if I know anything,
it's the burnt color of the brick
block after faceless block, the charcoal
steam from smoke stacks rolling
across the yellow backdrop of afternoon.
Soon we rattle over the tracks
and he points his Phillip Morris
at the roundhouse and switch engines.
Road dust rises from our back tires
and for a matter of seconds everything
disappears until we arrive to collect
mother from a room of long, dull basins
where a hundred women are washing
and wringing things out by hand
in the sweaty air. I wonder about
the women packed together all day
in steamy clouds, the fabric of silence
thick between them. And though
I have yet to give a single thought
to death, some vague and rainy climate,
some fear taken in with breath, pushes
in on me. . .yet somehow I am
almost certain that this ruined air
and sky, that narrow walk between
row houses leading to the one field
on Sunday mornings, cannot be all my life.

But Union Carbide has turned the tap water
black, and the daylight is so coated
with soot, I'm allowed outside only
a half hour at a time. Winter's grit
of light greys the river-basin town,
and the neon call letters of the station
where my father works nights

are an island afloat in hazy pink.
And equally strange to me by day
is his pre-recorded voice coming
through the silver grille of the radio
as he sits right next to me. Still, I can
recognize June Christy's silky vowels
whether the top is up or down, whether
I ever know who it was who ". . .came
a long way from St. Louie." Always I ride along
listening with my chin just over the dash,
looking up, thinking of cowboys roaming
that far and western expanse of sky.

And though on our cross-country move
I'm looking for the stars that fell
on Alabama, clapping my hands four times
to be deep in the heart of Texas, though the radio
glows warmly up front like a half moon,
I'm sound asleep in the back by the time
1952's sheen of lights spreads around L.A.

Outside Ventura, along Highway 101,
I wake to a breeze of orange trees
and salt air flooding in the wind wings —
on the ocean there's moonglow
and white lines of surf like branch
after branch of blossoms, and then
above me, spanning the entire horizon
of the windshield, a blue deep sky humming
with the clear, vast breath of stars.

OLD SPANISH DAYS

Santa Barbara, 1955

At a parochial school on the riviera
I've been studying French — in blue shorts
and a white pressed shirt, I am polite
in two languages. But by summer I'm saying
viva la fiesta, though I've learned nothing
of the Spanish or the old days that have them
dancing across posters with fans, with roses
in their teeth.

        And so, in a sombrero
from Woolworth's, I walk with mother
from our apartment on Micheltorena —
her auburn hair in a pony tail, her black
espadrilles beneath a flared coral skirt.
Hot pink and red geraniums bloom on cue
in the August yards; a little swirl of wind
and dry palm fronds click like castanets.

We're going early to find a spot from where
we can see every float and flamenco dancer,
every band that stomps down State Street.
Father's working at KTMS, and all I care about
is being held up when the Cisco Kid comes by. . .
The palominos and their riders strut past us
spangled to their smiles, the sun repeating off
the silver-dollar saddlework.

        But I applaud
most a formation of rusted street sweepers
roaring at the end through the buildings' blue
shadows, crepe paper, and clouds of confetti.
Later, in bed, I look out at the sky sparkling
like the ceiling of the Fox Arlington Theater
with its appliqué of stars, with its facades
of Spanish balconies dreaming above the aisles.

And I drift off to sleep beneath a moon bright
in the sky as a lost piece of eight. Next year,
I will be in a band of pirates and caballeros
in the Children's Parade — we've learned a song
by heart, and in our high and reedy voices sing
"Cielito Lindo" as if it means the world to us,
though there isn't one in our group who really
understands the words.

ANOTHER PLACE AND TIME

Like an accordion, a plastic, penicillin-green
curtain stretched and cordoned off the room,
aluminum handles disappearing with a click
into the wall. Mrs. Hansen nodded behind
her bifocals as Theresa Mills stood unaspiringly
in front of the corkboard, bleeding crucifix,
and flag to read out loud the first chapter
from our Social Studies text, *The Modern Age*.

So it was in 6th grade that we were crowded
out of homeroom and found ourselves makeshift
in the auditorium, desks drifting crossways
on a white-capped sea of waxed linoleum tiles.
Schneider and Witucki fired rubber bands at her
bare legs as Terry syllabically stammered on
with Bosnia and Herzegovina, Gavrilo Princip
and Archduke Ferdinand, all that unfathomable

intrigue of the Serbs. We were told to follow
silently along despite the pear-yellow afternoon
streaming through the transoms and washing out
the blackboards, the Palmer Method rules there
for our lives. But already I was falling behind,
waylaid by that fragrance of new books opening —
sawdust and apples — that fresh and acrid scent
saying again there was a world to make sense of.

Then a chapter heading picturing a metropolis
had me, and I was lost among people scrambling
in hats and suits; Hudsons, Nash Ramblers, and cabs
down the avenues; skyscrapers the color of coffee
with cream, lifting themselves above the streets
like diagrams of every declarative sentence.
But overhead, in a bleached distance of sky, a plane
climbed calmly, the only thing up there besides

some tissue-paper clouds. *The Spirit of St. Louis,*
I thought, shined-up and steady as the past, single
bright tune of an engine crossing the marvelous
world. And each time I opened that page in class
or in my mind, I could just make out a peaceful
hum, that silver square of wing pealing away
forever in the faint, blue atmosphere, sustained
on that light, from another place and time. . .

WALKING OUT THE APPIAN WAY PAST THE CIRCUS OF MAXENTIUS

If remembering another life
you find yourself familiar with the trees,
and the old road opens with shadows
that lift into the heat and haze
and out-distance the traffic's charivari,
then these arches will break off
mid-sky, like letters in a fragment
wholly untranslated by the blue.

And then that very umbrella pine
your Latin text opened to
over half a life ago,
and flame-tipped cypresses
green beyond the eternal
dismay and undoing of the air
hold themselves along the way
almost in conjugation, as if someone
had just stood up to say *amo, amas, amat.*

And you continue on for hours,
for that old love and its ruin
in statues on the roadside tombs.
And one young man whose features are fair
greets you, as if from a patrician box
overlooking the games, and, with good will,
another points the way into the world's bad heart,
unaware of the hour's decline,
the failing of an empire
and the blood.
          And their eyes
stare down the road where dust
softens the vacant hum of light,
and so could as easily gaze
upon the trees of Paradise
as on these burnished pines,
yet look for all the world
as if there is still a little
something to be desired.

II

Here I am again, two stories up making a little peace
at the level of the trees — the Cherimoya and Chinese Elm,
Podocarpus and Digger Pine — pointing out the air's thin hands
as they twist Italian cypress into wicks, into green torches
touching off the blue.
                        And though I can tell cobalt blooms
of ceanothus from sky-pale plumbago, it's a little thing I do,
favorably disposed as we are to light, like the flaming nasturtiums
or the fragrant frangipani.
                        To open to something on its own terms,
to speak its name, is a good place to start up the ladder of desire —
and so, when asked, I say I do this to take advantage of everything
I don't fully know, to take in equally the self-satisfaction of clouds,
the almost perfect sorrow of rain, given the light's sealed lip,
given the old need to account for ourselves under the sun.

*

Scientists scrape down stratas, through the calcification of time,
past a galaxy of shells, to star-silt, coal, and pinpoint
the ash of dinosaurs, the final days when creatures last lumbered
beside the palm trees, choking to death on the cold and dark.

It is a little thing we do, but what to make of these shed skins?
Surely we can learn from bones the dull lessons that would soon quit
our every breath, now that we can undo it all, take everything back
down to that first echo, the first disassembled dust?
                        Here I have it
otherwise a while, and take time to commend our orchard oriole,
the rogue pack of wrens picking apart the verbena, or the young cat
as she steals onto the roof of the storage shed for a better view —
how attentive they all are, how sure and sudden in their lives. . .

*

At 7 or 8, behind schoolrooms during lunch, I admired the windy lace
of acacias and lay among wild fennel and ivy locked into the anonymity
of the air, spelling out the silky progress of clouds. And I was not
thinking then of angels or of the shapes of beasts, but of the slow drift
of time keeping its counsel above me — the cataracts of light through limbs

revealing such riches as there were while we held onto our small place,
glorious and indifferent among the weeds.

Why do you do what you do?
is a question raised each time evening empties itself of light,
each time the sky rehearses its arpeggio of stars and signals you
to assume your place with or without some small verse of hope a life
might add up to.

The world is equally at a loss, but there you are —
you can take up its troubles, its bundle of sticks, you can turn away
forsaking even the wind's mute prayer — or you can praise it beyond
all your means. There are few choices, and no matter what you choose
to love it is a little thing you do. So after a time there is no reason
not to wear your heart out on these white sleeves. . .

THE LOST CATECHISM OF THE CLOUDS

Santa Barbara, 1957

And early to school those days
I wandered across the morning
yard in fog, a cloud of it so dense
that I went ahead on rote, guiding past
tetherball and flag poles as Korngibal
and Villa-Senor goaded from the invisible
safety of the steps — they called out
to trade wheat bread for white, to copy
catechism answers for class.
                              Sun burned
through by 10:00 and the priest popped in
to quiz us on the holy order of the words.
We opened the blue books from Baltimore
beneath our desks while another was grilled,
or we stalled looking up as if the sound-proof
tiles might open or the halo of lights above
our empty heads provide a clue to
Who Made You? Why Did He Make You?
Name the Five Near Occasions of Sin.
Then that fog floated out of each of our minds
as we stood to recite the impossible compound sentences
of God.
            Suffering that, we so loved ourselves
that nothing more than an updraft of wind
across the playing field would have us
feeling free and self-contained, and finally
we would drift in packs to the beach
running the creek spill to the flashing tide
and there in our indolence refute grammar
and the formulas for grace until dusk
with its half-light flayed above the western bluffs
found us late and heading home.

That year in Science we learned about
the monarch butterflies clustering here,
their wings wedged-in with dull eucalyptus
leaves, ready to slip-stream to Mexico,

to breed beneath an undimmed, winter sun
until warm currents rose again and they floated
north, dying to return. Still, we had no idea
how the unrehearsed sentences of their wings
could tell the proper avenues of air — bright clouds
of them releasing faithfully to nothing
more than wind, dissolving into the light,
into the blind perpetuity of the blue.

GIOTTO'S "ST. FRANCIS PREACHING TO THE BIRDS"

They've arrived at his bare feet as calmly as the poor
who have come to expect the flayed habit from his back.
They attend in pairs — the way it was once said souls first
were made — indifferent to the one tree standing for all
knowledge here on earth, and from which they cannot eat.

Magpie, goose, and crow; sparrows in their impoverished
suits; heron, rooster, and descending doves, have shaken
loose of skyways and cloistered bush to feed in the aura
and flat blaze of evening. But his extended hand offers
a blank perspective, and so they consider the intangible

kingdom of prayer, seeing that bread will not fall
to them all their days, that finally this burnished glow
might be every reward, all there will ever be beyond
the invisible example, the finite comfort of his words —
"Brethren, lesser cherubim, true apostles to the trees,

so that you shall be spared a degree of faithlessness
in this world, I reveal to you these wounds, the drab
roses and candle ends of my arms, the last things I have
to celebrate the explicit ecstacy of air . . . feast then
on this sparsely flavored dust, and doing so, be restored

to the bright dominion of wind. Go as our good reminder
above the confabulating leaves, the glorious and simple
sign of your wings admonishing the weight of our desires —
sing there the spirit unadorned, spellbound as smoke
rising into these gold and uncompromising fields of light."

SELF-PORTRAIT WITH WINTER

Santa Barbara

I must be 4 or 5, walking out of Woolworth's
with my mother; she's wearing a red cloth coat
for as long as I can remember — her auburn hair
in Bette Davis bangs and flip. And wondrously

across the air the McGuire Sisters are singing
"Silver Bells" — *it's Christmas time in the city.*
Strung over State Street's downtown lanes, three
bells glitter against the wind — I'm pointing

out the largest one when I'm tugged into a shop
of beige and pale-green dresses where I'll find
the one chair and sit politely while she looks
and finally buys nothing for herself. I have on

unscuffed Buster Browns, and my grey cap matches
my coat, so I match the swirl of sky which seems
grey all winter then. We hurry past pink faces
and packages, then somehow there's a peppermint

in my hand, and though rain could be on the way,
the world rushing by appears luminous and fine
as the store lights and street ornaments swell,
pushing back the early dark of a December afternoon.

*

I must have fallen in love twenty times since
blond Leslie Baldwin first kissed me on the bus —
I was 6 and my sleeping heart shot off like a kite
in an on-shore gale. And for all the intervening

moments, it must have been otherwise, looking
after clouds as if there were a destination for desire,
never the wiser for all my observations of the birds
patterning the wind, for all my climbing to the top

of pepper, pine, and cypress; jacaranda and acacia,
eucalyptus or oak. At least given that perspective
I survived an education at the hands of the nuns
and priests who consistently downplayed the earth.

One of the last clear things I remember is throwing
paper planes at the same bright girls still standing
in the weekly spelling bee, or that birch sapling
snagging the axle of my two-toned Chevrolet Belair —

I'm on my way home from the dance, wheels spinning
in mid-air over the arroyo; the next thing I know,
I'm turning in another semester's worth of grades,
closing in on 40, each year more like that feeling

when the brakes fade to the floorboard heading down
a breakneck hill in San Francisco, the dead weight
of your life hurtling toward the dark and implacable
gravity of that sea, sidewalks impossibly crowded

so nowhere to pull over, nothing to ricochet off
and stop — a cascade of faces, the slow and distant
motion of cars on the bridge rising softly into light,
and you can only hold your breath so long. . .

*

Still, after a time, we move on, much like the clouds
transformed by every recurrence, every happenstance
of light — and even when visiting, take the incidental
to heart against the measure of everything passed by.

Take the first autumn rains, just afterwards, walking
in the fermenting air of the Tuileries, a last yellow splash
of chestnut trees against a gossipy grey, men back at boules
as I stroll Rue de Rivoli with a street-bought umbrella,

while my friends a block up from the Mosque, pause
on their landing at three flat *blaps* clicking off the cold
length of the street and the holy man falling in his door —
the blood and purple wreath of flowers soon undone

across dark paving stones. What was there for any of us
to do but take our place alongside the steaming trees
and frost in the Jardin des Plantes, our breath's secret codes
going out toward the vanishing point of the promenade?

Then there I am at Pere Lachaise bundled to the teeth,
the cold sleeves of wind lifting next to nothing through
the stripped limbs as I trace the great rain-blunt letters
of Modigliani's name, and that young woman again

in her thin, black skirt going around, picking up
twigs between the graves. On the other hand, we're
at La Coupole eating shellfish from a pyramid of ice,
buying lamb and paté like bons vivants on Rue Monge,

on Rue Mouffetard for couscous, for beaujolais. Or there
I am above this town at a parochial school, learning my first
song in French, my mother coming by at lunch to console me,
wearing her one red coat, saying everything will be all right,

I should take my nap with the others, though I fear
the dark and shapeless currents of sleep especially
while there's sun. Then here I am, turning my desk lamp
off, looking out on a deep screen of blue, the outlines

of solitude that stars unveil where we see ourselves
subtly in the drifting sprays and dots, but no more
clearly, no more surely than when we are looking back
to that air-brushed wash of the past. Our atmosphere,

I've read, so clouds our vision that it's as though
we're staring up from the bottom of a lake; still we
go on trying to picture everything that separates us
from that light, that love, and are steadily drawn in.

THE INVERSE SQUARE LAW OF THE PROPAGATION OF LIGHT

(with apologies to Carl Sagan)

Leaves are splitting free in the invisible,
random winds as the last of the daylight
wears down. We've walked to the bluff
where evening, by turns, is immense
with that deep and airy blue, where stars
begin to slide in and then come set,
sterling in their old, unsolved equations.

The scientist tells us there are a few
hundred, billion stars in the Milky Way
alone — Red Giants, black, imploding holes.
But I like how the bushmen of Botswana have it —
the galaxy is simply the backbone of the night,
brilliantly holding up the sky.
                                    And just so,
Aquinas in his elaborate lock-step soul
would agree in so much as he saw that
all nature complements grace, and thus
went as far as you could go on Faith.
Just as abstract particles are not flung
into the sky to come down meshed cogs
and clocks, we might sift through
the velocity of Time and arrive at how
unlikely it is that we're just a splash,
haphazard in the cosmic pond — the stippled nebulae,
those scintillating bytes, may well add up,
connect like synapses in a mind.

The interstellar medium then
(read *dust*) sings brightly forth
in our bones, and the great, blind degree
and piecemeal of the void could well be still
swimming out from that initial spark.
And, given the unthinkable removes of light,
earth is as rare and predictable
a spot as any to be magnified against
the incoherent backdrop of the dark.

Although it includes everything that is
forever lost to us, it is with us always,
stored in the mists of light we think of
as the mind, those loose atomic stanzas
that replay our lives disproportionately
against the dark.
        It is all that becomes
of us and there is little we can ever do
for it when it blurs away at the edges
like scars, like old films, like the slow
lace of floss the body whitens to. . .

And though the universe, like an infinite
concertina, continues to expand on its one,
steady note, it must, according to all we know,
sooner or later fade out — there may well be
other music wherever it is we are not, or are
no longer.
        Nevertheless, we endure, reverberate
long enough to hear that out by Proxima Centauri
Cronkite's "You Are There" or "Person to Person"
with Edward R. Murrow is just now beaming in
through the snowy interference of space. Likewise,
by the time the whorls about Beta Pictoris collapse
to planets, those same years of light which left
our hands long ago will arive with Murrow
inhaling a Chesterfield as incisively as ever,
that omniscient cloud of smoke still drifting
around him in immutable black and white.

And in the early 60s the Nightly News reported
that a homeowner in the outskirts of Texas
tuned in broadcasts no longer on the air,
original transmissions of "Ernie Kovacs"
and "You Bet Your Life" pinballed off
asteroids, bounced sadly about the moon
before returning in our own, inimitable image.

This being so, my friend's stories of his family
make infinitely more sense — great aunt Stella
Funston, saxophone for the all-women orchestra
from Melbourne, sailed to Colombo, Ceylon,
in 1925 and played the Grand Hotel; he saw them
standing alongside their instruments, glowing
in floor-length gowns, in that hazy white
and brown of early photographs.

                          There's the ice
at the Pan-Pacific Exposition, 1906 — and at 18
his grandmother is a champion figure skater
from Australia; his grandfather is strolling
San Francisco's Legion of Honor in his best
linen suit, a doctor on holiday from El Salvador —
he lights his cigar and is momentarily blinded
by a dazzle of silver zigzagging off the rink. . .

This rhapsodic miscellany inevitably concludes
with him stepping right out of the blue,
through the door at a fixed point in time
to tell me all this — months since I saw him
off to wander the outlands of Mexico, south
of Michoacan.
                The days string out now
and luff toward the sea with the dusty waves
of heat; we take our fruit juice and rum,
our talk, out on the terrace beneath the fading
copse of camphor trees, early moon and evening sky,
all of which shine secondhand but, like us,
appear to be unchanged, as far as we can tell.

III

EXTEMPORE

Non in tempore sed cum tempore Deus creavit ordinem mundi

for Luis Omar Salinas in Fresno on the occasions of his
50th birthday and the publication of his selected poems

Heat and humidity, the days
reshuffle and stick to our backs.
And although the beatific clouds
acclaim us and rose petals may still
shower mystically into our laps,
I have given up on stars,
that bright algebra of threads,
any number of which may have thinned
to nothing and returned
to the soundless registration of dust.
And I have given up on the dead
in their carbon dated shoes, who,
like all of us, are in need of a little
quiet conversation against the night.

A little history tells us
the pomegranates will abound by Fall,
but we are at a loss to recall
those philosophers whose fruit
they are — but clearly the one
who proclaimed that everything was fire,
rarefied and condensed, was on to something.
Even Einstein would not tell us all —
though he explained about acceleration,
about age in relation to speed and light,
our bodies part and parcel of the split
infinitive of time.
                    And what is this
to us, my friend? It is everything
we take for granted, from the elementary
iambics of the heart to the free forms
of cottonwoods in wind, bits of sunlight
strung leaf to leaf as if, like us, the trees
had angels guarding the blue surrounding
the empty strophes of afternoon.

At evening, there is the code
of clouds and we know now to interpret
what short or long hopes of it we can.
We have a tableau vivant of sun-strafed hills,
the dry procession along the road of oatstraw,
of thistles with their bleached crowns looking
as bald as Giotto's monks. And you
find yourself in this stilled life
walking up to your childhood house
and memory standing there in your
mother's flowered dress.
                                    And this is why
perhaps, we tend toward love, and failing that
toward a heaven as invisible as our breath,
as invariable as the horizon's half-dollar moon.

Think of early May, a little moisture riding
the air out toward Fowler or Firebaugh,
the tense spiky greens of vineyards,
the winnowed day-stream dipping down
among the rows, among the workers
gleaning fields who let it touch them
the way grace and joy cannot.
You can step out there and let that light
become you, for when one day
you take that trip to Ecuador
and at your leisure climb
Mt. Chimborazo, there'll be no need
to know anything about the meek
as you look across the high plateaus
and in that day mist see how everything is
leveled, left off again to imagination. . .

And if we only shine out here, indifferent
finally to our fate puzzled through the elms,
we may yet take on significance in relation
to the earth. Let night pass like a silent bird
even though "Por Una Mujer Casada" has drifted

too often from your windows, for the world
is content to have you whistling rancheras
on your way back from town, or rising early
to appraise the bounty of fields.

                              It may help too
to remember that even though Van Gogh promised
portraits of all the saints, he left only
the holy painting of his chair, and thereby
gave dignity to the poverty of the little thing
we choose to do. And so you're called
to the tasks of solitude and dream as across
the fields and abandoned lots a few lines rise
with the smoke from your cigarettes,
from the record player to the stars
where Jorge Negrete still sings, where you
see that sparkling city in which you again
stroll the avenues in a suit and hat
humming a tune from the music hall
and are mistaken by girls waiting near
the exit for the Star as you pause to light
a smoke, your actor's good looks illumined
there for a second, your good eye cast
toward God, if he's awake above
the neon and sentimental fog of the times.

So while in our youth we thought
it was enough to gaze up devoutly
in our white shirts, it never was —
and whether you make a pilgrimage to the sea
again or not, and walk the promenades
admiring the bar lights and the passers-by,
time from the very first, has been running
out, though our prayer has always been
to make something of it, to have a life
that outlasts the trees — and while this seems
a reasonable request, the crows clatter overhead,
knowing better as they cut into the blue.

All the same, see if a poem doesn't find you
after wandering all day about town,
at your favorite cafe taking iced coffee
and milk, making notes on everything
that's left to glitter mutely in the afternoon,
tapping some perspiration from your brow
with a new silk handkerchief, when she asks
to share your table — you'll give in quickly
to joy, and as long as you're working like this
all will be well, and it will be all right to forget
the swelter and sadness of days, the fact
that the years have told us little about love —
only, it seems, about art and work —
and after all this time the only difference,
the only ease, will be that the images come
more quickly, apparently from nowhere —
death too, one day, will arrive like that.

CLOUDS IN SUMMER

Heaven and earth are ruthless. . .

Lao-Tse

Small patches of quiet now, shade standing
in pools — heat scours the trees, and birds
are afterthoughts in the slumbering air.

From the cliff it is clear to see across
the channel to five clouds cast adrift above
the five islands, and beyond where they roll

off into the azure curve of everything,
renouncing wisdom, surrendering the world —
these among the many least things to the wind.

*

And before the slapdash dusk dies out
and the blue evening unbuttons her stars,
sea mists ride the horizon's blanched raft

giving up those last ghosts of light —
then, in the south, the Magellanic Clouds
bloom like the white carnations of memory,

those could even be lovebirds calling in the palms
as, with the moonrise, a mackerel sky swims up
like small fish lured by a lantern to the top.

*

Past two, and below here all the workers
and musicians, even the new lovers
are probably asleep, leaving this bright city

to the undreaming and recalcitrant clouds,
those mare's-tails trailing their foreign
inflections, their adages and intimations

concerning the enterprise of this life, the sum
of every emptiness they have seen, slipping
between heaven and earth all their days.

*

They are only the airy substance of themselves,
not unlike our astral bodies then, which forget
us, fretting the shimmering piecework of light

while we lie cold as leaves with our desires
assuming each turning of the sky will come
to more than the simple clockwork of earth,

which, despite the piety in loss, reaches back
to carry the implacable past along, glimmering
vaguely as stars or salt on the surface of the sea.

*

Days drift by no more than blossoms down river,
everything finding its way out of our arms —
and so I think of Lao-Tse, who, sick at heart

with the ways of men, went riding off
into the desert to die, yet was persuaded
by a gatekeeper at the frontier to write down

the enigmatic, cloud-like body of the Tao
so that we might understand, stand under it
finally, without any thoughts for ourselves.

PLAYING FOR TIME

for Gary Young

We're walking down Grant through Chinatown,
and the sun's worked free of summer fog.
We have a few days off, are in love with the frivolous
industries of living. We eat char schiew
and sweet bean cakes on the street, browse
the Paradise Bazaar for all the useless fiddlesticks
we can afford, having more or less made it
through our mid-30's.

     And because we have
few illusions about our place in the world
of letters, we slip into the LI PO, built out
to the sidewalk like a river cave and easily
as dark. We drink fashionable Tsing Tao
though there's plum wine, Three Snake Liquor
above the bar, but also pinball in the back,
red plastic lanterns and news on the portable TV —
somehow they knew we were coming. . .

In a minute, our eyes adjust and we discover
an ancient, life-sized painting of the poet
at our backs — beneath a bare cherry tree,
he accepts a cup of wine, small honor
and greeting for his journey; and despite
the poverty of his station, he is as serene
as the thin clouds, content with the little
thing he does.

    And to show that such illustrious
establishments are named for poets, we take a photo
at the door before sauntering down the block toward
what sounds like vintage jazz some shop's cranked up
to draw a crowd — but it's two men, impromptu on guitar
and sax, astride milk crates playing "Body and Soul"
as silky and sure as the peach-colored negligee
stuffed in the sax's mouth,

which mutes and mellows,
keeps the cops away. The other fellow fingers
a beat-up steel string as effortlessly as if he'd taught
Barney Kessel how to chord. They lay it down
easier than that buttered pearl of a sun dipping west,
sweet as a breeze, cheap as it comes, and we have to
wonder why we're the only ones stopping to drink
it in, to drop a dollar onto the worn fur of the case.

They are too fine, steady and full of that
blue river and resolve of jazz to be playing
for drinks; certainly too little in it for dope.
We tell ourselves this must only be the world,
oblivious by turns and late in the afternoon,
and this is nothing if not the best there is —
place to place for supper, for dignity after
a bad job's kicked the daylights out of you.

They slide into Ben Webster's "I Got It Bad
and That Ain't Good," hit his flutter beyond
the last note, his after-riff, the signature of the man
inside yet outside the evanescent body of the song —
that wind-beat releasing its heart-tight breath,
phrasing balanced on the air like clouds on light. . .
just playing to put something real between
their four good hands, just playing for time.

TO GIORDANO BRUNO IN THE CAMPO DE' FIORI

Giordano, it's fall in Rome, overcast
for days where the sun was the only
science you were content could save us —
that primal grist we were spun about
as surely as the gold and quintessential
pears which reappear along summer boughs.
Old heretic, you were dead right
about the new astronomy, but the papists
wouldn't suffer the least celestial truth
and sent you to the flames for the fire
of your philosophies, for defying doctrine
and their dark ages, and, they thought, forever.

The century went forward on all fours
but the intricate, white architecture
of your thinking went begging until
it was bluntly cast into this statue
as overlooked here as the irregular sophists
who gather beneath it at dusk to share
some vino da tavola and recite
the last anthems of the flowers. . .

Nevertheless, old firebrand, I remember
that a principle is suspired in it all,
in the dark and in our dull hearts,
in the pearl-like apotheosis of stars,
for tonight your weather-beaten outline
looms above the square as ragged
as one of the lost continents
of the moon — and across the pitched
or spired roofs, the shadow of your
infinite idea rises with the mists
like a blue wing over the bluer sky.

Tomorrow, no doubt, we'll come again
from the Midwest for exchange rates,
the ruins and the partial restorations
of romance; we'll believe without question

and so run no risk from the church.
But there's a new inquisition here,
sectarian as the old — it takes us away
from lunch under bright umbrellas
and unsettles conversation over drinks
along the Via Veneto; this red brigade
would kneecap half the globe to get
their way. So maybe it's as you say —
after all there is no real evidence
of change, and these Calvinists of anarchy
as well turn a blind eye to the eternal,
and, in the fashion of the day, would not
hesitate to dump your body in the trunk.

And those who saunter by each hour,
with shopping bags and the *International
Herald Tribune,* wake one of us in his sleep
and he'll swear that Spinoza, your schoolboy
who stole the thunder and the themes,
pitched for St. Louis, possessed
a wicked slider and good control.
Who among us cares for the incandescence
of the spheres reified in our bones,
a plurality of worlds?
                              And even though
Aristotle declared nine windows to the soul,
they all reflected the extravagant clouds
or nothing more than that first cloud
Plato knew half beyond this life,
the wind-blue lake all souls float down from
with perfect knowledge of the trees —
so you divulged memory's thirty seals
and the geographies of the astral plane.
For this they gave you a robe of ash
and made you master of the clouds.

But Bruno, great speculator, where
in the long thought of God are you now?

Was there no thread of salvation
in throwing the sanctimonious dogs a bone
of contention, in having recounted
one illustrious atom of Unity?
I still sit out tonight thinking it through,
raising yet another Campari-soda
in your barely recovered honor, not ten feet
from where you disappeared in smoke.
I'm waiting for the low haze to lift,
for my blood to sing a little.
Didn't you, when tied to the stake,
sense the pull of the dead planets,
the immense absence beyond your skin?
And each day now, what do you make
of this marketplace with the last
fruits of the season, the flower stalls,
olives and bread, the pungent cheeses?
All day long I make compromises
between body and soul: a bit more
asiago on the gnocchi, less red wine
after 10:00 — and what I want to know
grand necromancer, is if finally
any of it is any use?
                    But regardless
I'm here to appreciate September nights
mystic as your gaze across the campo,
or the mute liturgies of stars appearing
at last and spinning like every petal
of fire that took you up, boundless
as belief. Can it truly be, once
and for all, all the same to you —
your bones left to the white heat
of ignorance, forsaken even as these stones
in the piazza are foresaken — this planet
coming to grief over the insubstantial
word? Do you still hold that flesh is
nothing more than the blossom of time,
of ash, and that it will fall away

before this incarnate light? That it's
all radiance *and* all dust? Or here,
on this very spot for all these days,
have we been merely treading air?

HALLEY'S COMET FROM THE WEST COAST, MARCH, 22, 1986

for Victor Kogler

From the promentory we could hear the dark
arrhythmic break of waves drum the silence
of the early air — then the oil platforms
like an armada, lit and busy in the bay.
We expected every light, all life to be down,
but even this sleepy town did not completely
sleep. Nevertheless, we held out our arms
and measured our blind palms against a gone
horizon line — two up and five to the right —
and there fished about with the naked eye,
halfway down from Mars, for that motionless,
white swish of dust . . . Nothing.
We stood there momentarily stunned
by the light-tide of the Milky Way — that still spin
and irrepressible smudge of its flung grains —
and tried then to pinpoint the stars shifting coolly
to hang there with the thread and bones of all our myths.
We went to binoculars, seining below that lake
of light and caught it there streaming away
in its own bright floss, sinking in the slowed
motion of space like an Independence Day sparkler
in a smoky night's display, deep and south
of wherever it is we are.
                    My friend recalled
the only time he saw such a wonder was 1956,
his mother rallying the family at 3 am onto
their lawn in the flat heart of San Fernando —
and from there they could see plain as day,
and without binoculars, a raw flash and radiance
surge all the way from the Nevada Test Site,
cannonball across the western night, and then
pulse out.
          The sky was neither blue nor black,
no hour we knew outside the fog of dream —
but there we were, frozen at that clear
point where all perspective breaks down
with just such a first and last long look out.

How little
does justice
to the thin air
and the height
of the cold, except
perhaps this needle
in the blue — where
before there was
no means for clouds
to abrogate their duty
for filling sky in
a beautiful way, there
is now this span of open
lattice work, spun space
to space, erasing absence
and coming to a point.

And rising
up inside
it seems knitted
with the intuition
of birds with whom you
share the view and feel
that vertiginous breeze
rifling the gold buds
of birch trees, driving
the swans like white petals
across the slate ponds below.

Wrought iron
was strung up
in the substanceless
abstraction of thought,
set somehow against all
the trips and balances
of nothing, the engineering
of the air. Above
the pylons he arched

the shrinking heavens
with girders resembling
an aviary or pergola,
then figured out
the twelve thousand pre-
fabricated parts, the 2½
million (more or less)
rivets in their bare
and steely sequence,
and so turned aerodynamics
around on a curve
of quadrilateral legs,
cross-braced so precisely
that the bending
and shearing predilections
of wind were steadily
transformed to forces
of compression
so even in the hypothetical
troughs of a hurricane
there would be less
than nine inches sway.

Knowing how
an effect diminished
uniformly from a point
this master of bridges
out-wondered the changing,
free-fall rivers of the sky.
Against gravity, and with
the foregone and unbending
resistance of the cognoscenti,
he elevated the function of iron
in the world, and clearly saw
how it would accommodate this
impending and audacious grace.
Even a modest office emerged —
a nest on the final terrace

for the uncluttered atmosphere
of work, complete with wireless,
telegraph, a glass lantern on top
to clock the advances in weather,
and also with chairs, a table,
fine glasses and Veuve Clicquot
chilling for the two times Edison
would share this rare altitude,
this bright fabric of the mind —
this, the first sound place where
you could stand back a little and
gain a degree of perspective, a place
from which you could praise, almost
objectively, the handiwork of the earth.

IV

OCTOBER VISITING

Fresno, 1985

for Jon Veinberg

*Even if I were certain that I was going
to heaven, I would pray God to let me go
by the longest possible route.*
                                    Nikos Kazantzakis

Again, what great good it does
to go among these fallen leaves,
through retiring alleyways
of a sturdy merchant class,
admiring the fragrant dog roses
as they fail along a fence
and in this remind myself about beauty
despite the flush perfumes of death —
all this on the way to my friend's
porch where we'll sit among bouquets
of japonica and orange, a midday sun
through a smoke of musty sycamores.
Perhaps we'll take an early drink
for I think it was Po Chu-I, old poet
and governor, who found leisure solely
during ill health, and who wrote
how high office only profits others.
So today we'll praise the essential
precept of idleness, and for a while
do what we do best — sit here
absorbing light, watching the air move,
speculating on the apparent infinities
of space or whether there might be
violoncellos playing in the foggy woods
of an afterlife. Or, more reasonably,
we might consider that wisdom
in the patience of clouds,
tireless and at peace with change
but which, when rushed, are likely to leave
all their old furniture lying in the road.
And how can we overlook the apples

weighing down the waxy boughs
while these long days unwind, for always
I find myself envying everything about
the trees — their drowsy contemplation
of the earth, and yet how all their lives
they are pulling purely away from it.

Last fall along the Arno
white spume lifted from the weir
as we climbed inside Brunelleschi's duomo
and then plant-like out the top
into the *Sfumato*, that tea-rose pollen
of light which floats there thick
enough to tempt you to also try
and take the air, give yourself over
to that surge and longing, to the lilac
clouds which somehow promise neither
happiness nor rain.
                But rain found us
in Rome with dogs lagging aimlessly
behind in the streets as we walked
all afternoon to the cemetery,
rang rust from the bell, circled
and rang again, yet no one came
to spit a curse onto the walk
for the weather or our English.
So, without seeing where he's not
quite buried, or if the hand
of water has worn away his name,
we left unable to place our two sticks
of good intent together among the stones,
came away with wet leaves stuck
to our shoes, a wind knifing the blue
junipers with the unfinished
music of an ode.
            Then Lerici
and Cinque Terre, the steep vineyards
and airy slopes of an ethereal, white wine.
Or a Vino Santo below the lights

of Villa Marigola where they read
Byron in Italian three nights running,
where we were lulled, indolent as those
red or green skiffs nodding on the bay.
And along the breakwater that morning
we watched divers winch up a sailboat
with a broken mast — and took a last walk
to the point where we looked south
as far as Viareggio where they fished
Shelley's body out, no longer able to sing
the sea out of its veins, and sent then
its smoke up with difficulty on the dank,
impassive air.
        And above us now
in Yosemite's cloud-high meadows,
hide-thick pods of milkweed
are breaking open of their own accord,
each with its white hosannas flying
on the short breaths of autumn — and if
there is another life and all our atoms
sail out likewise to a breeze, and if we
grow calm then, shining at some blue remove,
why should we now become preoccupied
and hurry to that insubstantial end?

Today, everything is before us, yet
invisible as the snow that will fall
in a week or two across the Sierras —
the road offers us our own grey dust
so there is no telling which way
to proceed — we could be closer to heaven;
we could be simply whistling our way out
of our skins. We have the fine nostalgia
of evening articulated in the ash trees
and for the time being we might do well
to emulate starlings in the high branches
for that last varnish of light
as they offer, without restraint,

their unmanaged choruses of faith.
For soon the days will draw short
and with them these opportunities
to eavesdrop on the convivial plants
and afterthoughts of wind; soon, we may
sit out after work with some red wine
and company against the cold, and the irony
of that light submerged in our bones
will surface nonetheless, and then
we will not be able to help looking up
at the rising tide of stars and feeling
the rush of all their old designs on us.

THE ARBORIGINES *IN THE JARDIN DES PLANTES*

for Sherod Santos

Barely arrived for the last
of autumn, for that thick
daylight in stippled drifts
through a ginkgo's yellow fans,
for beeches going up
like the gods' lost fire —
and down the gravel promenade
the arch of tailored sycamores
vanishing to a point
in a smoldering haze.

We praised a persimmon tree,
its free-floating heaven
of auburn moons —
we praised the greenhouse,
Rousseau's equatorial palms,
the exorbitant atmosphere
sustaining the dark fronds.
Yet each day found us
before a gate to that stand
of woods, looking up to see
which of the life-sized
molds of men and women —
infused so they'd photosynthesize
and turn longingly toward the light's
blanched heart — still held
amidst the tutelage of leaves;
and which, giving up the spirit
of those breathing days, climbed on
out of themselves, no more finally
to the sky than smoke unthreaded
against the wind-sheared grey.

When only two or three still clung
by something as impenetrable
as faith, we turned and left them
where a few chartreuse sprays

still managed to pick some life
from gusts, left them with their heads
listing a little to one side —
a slow study for the absent blue —
but looking as though they might
at any moment succumb
to the river mist and drowse;
or perhaps, we silently agreed,
as if listening, as if
the thrummed stations of the air
were fully invisible with wings.

LAST NIGHT AT AKROTIRI

for Nadya

As if this were a place where omens still held
sway, white pigeons were landing atop the blue-
domed roofs then lifting off again.

Up the coast, the headland's red pumice, stones
with their bleak information about the past —
terraced hillsides left to saltweed and thorn,
and broken hulks of windmills across a ridge
like a lost procession of angels.
                  The one hotel
was a stagger of cave-shaped rooms ascending
the bluff, each wall white and thick as the clouds
sleepwalking at midnight, there beyond the high,
small balconies.
             Below on the patio, we sat out
over pastitsio or moussaka, the local bottles
of Atlantis or Volcan wine glimmering amber
and green as early stars. We breathed easily —
so much work behind us, so much light yet to rise
effortlessly into our arms — no trouble it seemed
the Aegean's intransitive blue would not absolve.

And when, at two or three, Mr. Tassos' friends
from town finally tired of the ouzo, bouzoukis,
and whirling violin, I'd open our door for the breeze
and walk out alone among the tamarisks on the cliff,
fists of dirt and sand swirling over the edge, and there
watch for the passenger ship that slipped each night,
bright as a city, toward Crete.
                When it sank
beyond the sea's dark edge, I looked out further
to the fields of stars that too seemed abandoned
and spare. I thought back to the last Minoan here,
one unable to sleep, one who walked this path
for that faint reassurance off the running commentary
of waves just when all the earth shook loose beneath his feet —
and who, turning toward the south, looked homeward

as the apparent heavens broke free from their dark
ledge and showered down the fire that took up
a dreaming world into morning.

If it is true on earth
that nothing is ever
destroyed, but only changes
form, then Venice is, and
is not, of this world.
Its serried palaces float
airily across water,
the white and constant dome
of San Giorgio Maggiore
little more than a cloud
effect against the horizon —
and with every distance
of the air, the Byzantine
arches and marble spandrels
appear as insubstantial
as their reflections —
the whole of it awash
in the luminous, late slant
of autumn.
        And while islets
list serenely, and the sea
comes up over the *campiellos*,
the balconies and gold mosaics
of St. Mark's are shifting
a little like a loose
puzzle on a tray.
        Even so,
the piazza is rarely empty —
even in a snowy pre-dawn
when the sighs of white flakes
fill footpaths on the Rialto,
they are heading for Carnival.
And now as always, the shops
suggest their glass and coral
and masks — you might be
one in the torchlit throng
with a plum-colored Pulcinella,
its nose as long and rude,

as notorious as the centuries
dusting down from chandeliers
of the Ca' Foscari and flooding
a length of the Grand Canal.

You could be among the loiterers
in the Palazzo Ducale — late
afternoon, awaiting the pink
refraction of the sun
flowering across the facade,
or one disappearing through
the arcades to dice discreetly
at the ridotto, while above
on the altanas, among succulents
and chimney pots, ladies are still
out to sun-bleach their hair.

And in the near and distant
relations of this light
you drift easily
through the piazzetta,
your dark coat spreading
like a cape in the sea breeze
off the mole, and here you
almost recall who you were
all that time ago . . .you only
have to step into the gondola
and glide out on that green sea
to find yourself in procession
behind the Doge's Bucentaur,
the hundred oarsmen pulling
for the Lido, in La Sensa,
the Feast of the Ascension,
regatta and high holy day
commemorating the marriage
of Venice to the sea —
the chains of sunlight lifting
off the regiment of waves,

the fervent perspective
of the sky faithful to the last
irradiant edge of cloud.

PHOTOGRAPH OF MYSELF BY MODIGLIANI'S GRAVE, PERE LACHAISE, 1984

Not a breath of wind in the inarticulate trees, late
November, and by 4:00 the gauzy light above them
has already begun to fail, barely enough now
for photographs, one reason we've come to these

rococo tombs and stand about as bold as crows.
This small Babylon of hills wears away with dusk
and it takes little then to turn over the notion
of another world — that distance, say, pearled

momentarily through the threadwork of boughs
or, out of range of this ice-blue sky, some shining
rampart beyond these skin-grey scarps — especially
if you'd just dogged your fate and found yourself

delivered to the Costa del Sol, to drift weeks away
deep into October on a sherry-colored inlet and a bay
where shore birds skimmed the background music
of the waves, then lifted into the silk trees' gold ellipses. . .

We come to the austere and polished onyx of Proust,
an immoderate monument to Wilde with wings soaring
headlong for the rising night, which is overtaking
everything by the time we stop a student who can

point to Modigliani among a city block of graves
so dull, so even, they could almost be cement. . .
Amedeo who cherished stone, the spirit's shape un-
locked in it, the soul's thick dust, is marked here

by a dirt-poor slab, his name and date worn down
while the clouds killed time, much the way the black
weight of his luck undid his lungs and let the light go
from him like bees smoked out to an unredeeming

blue, the same insubstantial air Jeanne Hebuterne
fell through a day behind his death and so shares

this unaspiring space and love at last. And we,
touching these names, wish simply that whatever

flame remains will not die out of our eyes wholly
unremembered and without form. So when the photo's
snapped, I do not appear to be the visiting bon vivant
of modest ambition and comfortable luck — I'm only

somber in my Spanish coat, nonplussed in a red scarf
at my throat representing nothing more than warmth.
I am looking into the flash as if I still expect to live
forever, or as though I've at least discovered in the dark

at my back why, at 36, I've outlived his misery
and genius and can now walk ingenuously through
the world a little more unmindful of my age and old
shortcomings. And when I must take a plane back

across a winter sea, I can be consoled knowing that
no man's finally the man he would rather be. Thus
I'm flattered and pose gratefully before the dead while
these winsome stars circumscribe the night, obliquely

telling all, yet leave some room between them
for every death to come, for my abstract devotion
to clouds as if to some hope immured, as if this
unremitting sky held nothing personal against you.

Above here, there must be a swath of souls
wide and invisibly blue as this water,
and at evening I think they must drift through
the soft pinks and ambers of light,
still dreaming, and confuse their lives
with this one, as if some ash were still
swimming in the violet arc and afterglow —

for again, after dinner and the delicate,
straw colored wine, twilight thickens,
falls and filters out as auburn
as the skin of deer and fisherboys
Minoans left in frescoes on the walls.

Then, the dim taverna sparks with something
like clarinets and mandolins, an old melody
resonant and tenuous as joy; then the few birds
make no excuse for abandoning the trees,

and the young in one another's arms
take slight notice of this rich failing
of the light, or the old turning home in it
from the stony fields, hunkered from cutting
the clear grapes grown low and away from wind.

And once more I dreamed my body floating
hawk-like in its ease above the agate shores,
banking on thin air as the horizon roiled
in flame at the ocean's far end.
                              But when
you gaze up the sheer and volcanic cliffs
to villages ridged on the crater's lip
they seem no more than snow at an unknown height,
and a switchback toward them from the harbor
spirals like Dante's 50 rings, a whirlwind
of dust smoking upward from the quarried sand —